T0082787

Bowl Slowly

Inside Me

A poem buried in rubble
Obscure
Surely is deeper and
Sillier or
Conveying dim
Paths of
Long lost stars

Imperatives

Write or be vanquished!
Now cease or be anguished,
Always.

Milicent G. Tycko

authorHOUSE®

AuthorHouse™
1663 Liberty Drive
Bloomington, IN 47403
www.authorhouse.com
Phone: 1 (800) 839-8640

© 2017 Milicent G. Tycko. All rights reserved.

No part of this book may be reproduced, stored in a retrieval system, or transmitted by any means without the written permission of the author.

Published by AuthorHouse 10/21/2017

ISBN: 978-1-5462-1290-4 (sc)
ISBN: 978-1-5462-1289-8 (e)

Library of Congress Control Number: 2017915960

Print information available on the last page.

Any people depicted in stock imagery provided by Thinkstock are models, and such images are being used for illustrative purposes only. Certain stock imagery © Thinkstock.

This book is printed on acid-free paper.

Because of the dynamic nature of the Internet, any web addresses or links contained in this book may have changed since publication and may no longer be valid. The views expressed in this work are solely those of the author and do not necessarily reflect the views of the publisher, and the publisher hereby disclaims any responsibility for them.

Contents

Need a Sledge Hammer

The huge work had been accomplished a year ago. Decades of my various writings, which were piled in large boxes on my shelves, finally were woven into one book. In order to do this, I decided to use a few fictitious characters, describe their personalities, and thus give reasons for picking and choosing certain writings which would be subsumed within the story of each fictitious character. So there was created more than just a catalog of types of writings, or a chronological list of when the various writings were done. The first fictitious character was named Norma. She wanted to fastidiously clear out all the old shelves and be done with it, as she mused to herself. Within her story were phases of her long life and the writings, whether poems, essays, reflections, were coming forth, as if spontaneously, as she did her meticulous and well motivated work. Next I created another fictitious character called Maureen, who always wanted to avoid the dark hole of life, by doing positive and helpful things, and so little stories were invented to show her personality. The stories I wrote under Maureen's name were all based on actual stories from my own experiences. She was always frustrated, however, because she wanted to 'write a novel', and eventually she did face another story, a family story, that did lead to finality for her, she felt that 'at last she found how to end her novel'.

The big book I was writing also had to gather up lots of other essays I had written over the years, and so each was just placed after Maureen finished her novel. Luckily I did not have to edit these essays, and some I found very interesting as I went back to reading them years after I had written them. Some about writers, about a historic event, an opinion about societal changes. Not to be neglected, as this was one of my dearest favorites, was a children's story I had written, about a little horse called Tawny. The adventures of this beloved horse were inspired for me to develop, because at that time I had very young grandchildren myself, and knew they would enjoy it. Some other family members were also invited by me to draw some pictures which would apply to some of the chapters.

My book was published, first time I had ever published one, by accommodating and helpful people at AuthorHouse.com. Not a best seller, but has been read, and even appreciated, by some.

Now I want to have a sledge hammer, so I can return to when I did not feel it necessary to invent fictitious characters in order to incorporate my overloaded shelves of eons of writings.

With this sledge hammer, figurative of course, I have been extricating my poems and put them in one pile. Then, another pile has been made for the essays. Another for stories. This is all very satisfying to do because I feel I am returning to my real authentic self.

Hey, wait a minute. If anyone thinks this is an easy task, then they are not realizing that the style of that big book has made it cumbersome to relocate and extricate piles of separate writings. If a character was sitting alone and looking out the window at the snow that was falling, and then wrote a poem about it, how is one to bang and sledge and cut to just separate out that poem? I certainly am not in the mood to use a scissor and end up with heaps of scrap papers and then have to glue different pieces together for another onslaught. No way Jose. So I meditated for a while and then told myself that when making a separate pile of poems, it would be nice to leave the few words before and after the poem that might therefore give a cushioning of where and why that particular poem came forth. Just a few words, defined by whatever was on that one sheet of paper that also had the poem sitting on it. A flavor. No body had to wonder or review or imagine, often incorrectly, what the mood or the situation or the identity of people or thoughts expressed in that poem on that one page, really was. It was sort of a guide, and interesting incomplete guide, limited by that one page. At last I had solved my problem of using that helpful sharp and heavy sledge hammer to bang away at the sands of that big book to reach a particular poem. Likewise the same could be applied to bits and pieces of essays, or of opinions, or of rambling words that I now wanted to extricate.

So my desk and my floor and my nearby couch are cluttered with the bits and pieces from which occasionally rise up the brilliantly flaming poem, or essay, or story.

One of the insights I had written about in my big book, is that I never could actually stop writing. True indeed. I must now admit that there is a separated high heap of papers on my desk, about 11 inches tall already, that has brand new writings. Now and then I just write another few pages of a new topic that interests me. I use paper clips to separate one from the other, and do not feel that I ever have to do anything with this. On top of this pile I will now place my pages called Need A Sledge Hammer.

Bowl Slowly

I have been writing so much more stuff since my former book, called: Howl Softly was put together, so now I want to stuff these writings into another book. Problem is to find a suitable title. I tried: Howl Again but did not like this. Or perhaps: Howl Loudly but did not like this. After meditating in my typical critical fashion, I chose to relax last evening, on a cold night, after dinner, by watching some old movies. Since I loved seeing Paul Muni in The Good Earth, I looked for another of his movies, so many made. Scarface was the one chosen. Muni plays a totally different character in this notable early film about gang life in Chicago. He works his way up until he becomes the "boss" of a gang, during prohibition, that tries to defeat all the other competing gangs. Huge money involved, gorgeous apartments, girls, shiny robes, for the winning gangs. All carry pistols and some get hold of machine guns.

Paul Muni has other famous stars with him, such as George Raft and Boris Karloff. Well.....not to reveal the rapidly changing plot, at one point Boris is in a bowling alley, enjoying how well he bowls. The guys from another big gang have their eyes on him. Just as he has knocked down all but one of the pins, and then, with perfect aim expects to knock down the last standing tall pin, something happens. He is shot down dead by guys from the other gang. Maybe if he was not so confident and had not quickly tried to bowl down that last standing pin, but instead had thought it over slowly and waited to roll that heavy bowling ball for a long time, well, perhaps those other guys would have given themselves away by not expecting any change of Boris's rhythm. They would have wasted all their bullets, and by then, Paul Muni's gang would have these guys rapidly shot down dead. So.......sometimes it might be better to change your expected rhythm, and just Bowl Slowly.

p.s. So that is how I decided to title my new compilation of stuff: Bowl Slowly

Spring is Here at Last

After very variable weather in April, some days warm, some days chilly and rainy, and now it is May and we wondered if there would still be such disagreeable variety. Lo and behold it now is nice and warm and seasonable. Outdoor gardening and outside painting of deck and house can be done comfortably. Looks as if we have definitely 'sprung forward'.

So when it comes to outdoor weather, springing forward is desirable, at least now. But if one has the courage to let oneself be constantly inundated by the incessant repetition on radio, TV and Internet, about the political and economic events in our current world, then springing backward seems to be more sensible to me. It is easy for us older folk to reminisce about the good old days of yore. We did not have swifter than swift and smaller than small technical devices that relayed information, and focused on sordid information, quicker than a blink of the eye. So our media people had plenty of time to sort out stories and the unknown from known details, before broadcasting news to us. We could be gently prepared for the negative events to come, rather than being plunged into a boiling hot pool of undigested sordid information. We could also have recognized, though of course never completely honest, pundits help interpret the implications of these events upon our daily lives. Now we have a myriad of people anxious to tell us what to think, and often disinformation, or downright lies, are swirling from device to device and being thoughtlessly repeated by anybody at all who has access to one or more of these technical whippers.

If War was imminent, we were usually prepared by some authority figures to expect this and what would be required. Behind the scenes those figures first figured out what plans to propose outloud to their audience. Now we have hints of disaster, denials of details, new unconfirmed details, and louder and louder projection of all of this, which makes it feel, somehow, that those talking and perpetuating topics are mainly desirous of gaining personal fame, as actors and actresses. They are aware of innuendoes, how to sound like everyman, folksy, or pompous and know it all, or cute and sexy in putting forth horrible details.

In addition to all this confusing, deliberately confusing it seems, technical swiftness, the ethics and acceptability of topics has amplified unbelievably, so the behaviors and beliefs that in the past were unthinkable, and if rarely occurring were hidden quietly, have evolved to the point, well there is actually not a 'point' or end to this social sentence, where the world within and without is totally transparent. No stop signs. If outrageous then more doted upon and made to seem prevalent even if only a small percent occurs.

So, to me these cumbrously expressed thoughts and references all make me wish that in actuality we could 'spring backward'. There is a feeling of safety in this backward look at our world and at ourselves. There is complete mystery and foreboding in 'springing forward'.

The "Last Flower
of Summer"
"Flowering Story"
"Spring is Here at Last"
MGT

The "Last Flower of Summer"
From My Garden
MGT

Last Flower of Summer

The song about the "last rose of summer" kept me humming in late June, when our weather had just become officially summer weather, very hot and very humid and unpredictable rain showers. I enjoyed going out into my garden and viewing all the flowers that were now in full bloom. Those orange and tall tiger lilies that had taken over almost two thirds of my garden and two thirds of all the neighboring gardens. Since I myself am not orange and certainly not tall, always being the shortest girl in class, these wondrous tall, orange flowers enchanted me. They were so different from me, and therefore I could look up to them, rather than having to crouch down low to view and weed some of the other summer flowers that were popping out. Like the bushes and bushes of chrysanthemums, from which one is supposed to snip off the early buds, to make way for the late comers. The late comers were early this hot and humid day, and so there were already a few white chrysanthemum flowers and a few pink chrysanthemum flowers interspersed down there.

I did miss the lilac blooms, long gone, and also the peony flowers, long gone, which required me to snip off the brownish remains, so next year new ones would bloom better. I had also spent several hours snipping off the dead azalea flowers from the several pretty blooming azalea bushes in my backyard. I had varied colored azalea bushes, that gave me a big and lasting palette of color for weeks in late Spring. There was one particular azalea bush however, that was planted all alone in a more distant and shady part of the yard, and it always was the last one to bloom, pink flowers. By now, all of this late blooming azalea bush was definitely finished blooming, and a week before I had trimmed its little branches at their tips to make room for the next year of retarded blooming azalea flowers. Of course, the iris flowers were all gone and the iris leaves turning brown also.

This hot and humid day at the start of official summer, had me going outdoors early in the morning, to then be able to stay indoors in mid-day where the air-conditioners and fans and cold drinks could help me survive the heat. With coffee cup in hand, I went out to my deck and gazed around, humming to myself about the "last rose of summer" which was how I was feeling. I sipped and gazed around, and sipped and gazed around until my gaze reached the shadiest part of the yard, overcast with the branches of evergreen trees. I suddenly dropped my coffee cup, in astonishment. It was an almost empty cup, do not worry. There, on that late blooming azalea bush, was a large beautifully formed pink flower. It was surrounded by dark green shadowy greenery, and stood out proudly.

Now I changed my tune. I happily saw the "last pink azalea of summer".

This late and extremely gorgeous bloomer gave hope to all of us. Never say die.

Weaving With Neighbors

These last few days have been very busy since I started to weave again on a long forgotten loom which had been left down in my garage gathering dust. Most of my days had been suitably quiet for me. Only had to shop once a week for supplies for two of us. A few medical appointments to attend along with many of our peer group golden oldies. Walking my dog. That is about it. Not just any dog however. This one is an extremely active border collie named Princess, which we rescued from an animal shelter, have had her loving gratitude for over seven years. She does love to run swiftly all over our hilly backyard, and particularly when she sees anybody walking by. We are rather anonymous in our neighborhood, just quiet, docile, greying old folks. Many of the houses nearby have been sold to other younger folk and our kids are now adults who have blessedly given us six grandchildren by now.

Why did I have to find my old loom in the garage and dust it off now? We got a friendly invitation from the younger couple who have lived next door to our old house for almost ten years, and we did agree to visit them. We knocked at their door, a present of books in our hand, and then the neighbor man, a polite man born in London, and his wife, a lively Italian lady, greeted us with offers of drinks immediately. What a noisy crowd of other neighbors were already standing around the living room entrance. They carried drinks, from the buffet which had maybe forty wine bottles displayed, and rambled up to us, asking how Princess is doing. So they all knew our border collie. Not our names, but then we heard their happy stories and their hard luck sad stories. Since I am a listener type by birth, I asked a few pertinent questions and always heard a few dramatic essays back. One neighbor who had an old dog we knew, sadly told us that their dog had died a couple of months ago. Such a hard loss for them. My sympathetic frown though had to be quickly changed to a wide open smiling face when the usually silent neighbor who lived across from our house, came up to us and introduced us to his newly wed wife. In June they were married. I was weaving rapidly, my shuttle flying, the different colored threads making a cheerful, warm blanket. How great. So that lady I had seen going and coming near that house was a newly wed woman, and best of all, she had two dogs with her. No wonder Princess always barked through the fence when she saw them. They did ask how Princess was feeling.

A British relative and his wife then drew our attention. I started to feel blessed to know her. She had a beautiful daughter who had returned from Spain where she studied linguistics, and was now going back to London to finish her degree.

Today I again brought my loom to my room. This time the dust had vanished. The threads were tangled into a woven tapestry of thickness by phone I invited a few of these recently revealed neighbors to join in our home and meet darling Princess. Thick twisted threads were placed in my room. Near to the door. Upon hearing the knocks my fingers did twitch. I knew I would soon start to do neighbor weaving once more. They all galloped in, laughing and smiling and poured packages of gifts on my table. Not books. Wine bottles and packages of British mince pies. My own grandchildren greeted them smilingly and knew they would soon get to chat with new people. The oohs and the aahs flowed around and my loom was soon tracing the feelings with thick cheerful threads. The colors kept changing and quizzical indeed. Once they all had to leave, my Princess yelped helplessly and I told her that soon they would all come again.

Just look at the thickness I wove on my loom. Now sweet darling doggie, I finish the edges and soon. Yes so soon. Your blanket to lie on will fly from the loom.

Cars Can Talk

Recently I saw a pamphlet with the history of many cars and their photos. The first Model T and then Model A and then years later the little "bug" and then the big streamlined cars and the convertibles and the priuses of the world. Some topics seem to be dwelt upon endlessly, like cars, and then like dogs, and then like diets and then like healthy fitness, and then like myriad versions of yoga and tai chai and back to diets there are endless words about vegetarian diets and about vegan diets and about carnivores, well then back to the history of humans, back to early man and early pithecanthropus, and then about the deep ocean and the lost whales and sharks. But the history of cars seems to have a very special attraction. Inanimate products. No life of their own. Well, maybe.

My first car was actually a well used closed in truck that my father had used in his construction work for years, and was now ready to look for another second hand truck. It was a dark blue Dodge, as he favored Dodge trucks. It needed constant repairs but took numerous journeys with me and friends from downstate to upstate New York, where as college students in the snowy, cold, freezing campus of Cornell University, we felt blessed to be students that did have a car to use coming up and down between semesters and especially when the warmer days hit and we could easily chug along the woods and lakes nearby instead of always seeking a heated chair in the library. If there were scratches and bumps on the well-worn outside so what, and using the old fashioned stick shift and rolling the windows up and down by hand appealed to novice young drivers. The aroma of old paint cans and ladders and speckled seats were all artistic and I still felt part of my family when I sat in the front of this old truck which had transported many cousins and friends of mine over the years also. It was not only a one car family I grew up in, it was more or less a one car extended family as few owned cars living in a big city with bus lines and also trolley lines back then. Newark was easily a next door neighbor of Manhattan as it was easy to go there by bus to Port Authority or by catching the train to lower New York. This old blue Dodge truck took uncountable journeys through the Holland Tunnel to visit relatives in nearby Brooklyn, to see museums, to go to the Coney Island Beach, which could not yet be taught to pronounce Jones Beach. Not necessary since the boardwalk was fun for us kids to play under and if we were not afraid of heights some liked the Ferris Wheel. Not me. I liked hunting for jelly apples. This old Dodge truck was not single minded and often also drove us children and friends to the beaches at Staten Island where we used a big outdoor swimming pool while the grown ups sat upstairs in the covered two deck boardwalk, occasionally looking down at us and telling us to get out and dry off.

So, though an inanimate object, my first one with four frequently flat tires needing repairs, and with a simple stick shift and roll up by hand windows, makes my eyes tear and my heart leap with joy in memory of the years bygone and the generosity of my father in giving and trusting me with his well worn second hand blue Dodge truck.

Over a few years life did change and being just an undergraduate in the snow covered hills upstate was finished with. New studies, new friends, new adventures living in apartments in crowded Manhattan where nobody but insane individuals had a car. Subway lines and street buses and even the third-avenue L made getting about easy. Riding the third-avenue L does date me. Some idiots decided to tear it down, but at least it was well portrayed by artists Hopkins who found peering into dark windows and imagining the folk inside and looking down on shops and bunking knees with all the passengers was important for existence. Me too. Torn down and then so-called fancy shops and restaurants lined the street below, and pedestrians never looked up for the noisy third-avenue L anymore. They looked at store signs beckoning them in. They looked at each other rushing by on the sidewalks and they looked at the low to the ground vehicles with numbers on the front.

Having finished the growing up process, we were now two wedded people living uptown on the less expensive west side, where we could walk to see the Hudson River and get to our jobs and studies in mid-town easily. Admittedly there were cars now parked along our street. Park Terrace East, but people seemed to use these inanimate objects only when driving away, far away, from Manhattan. On vacations, on the new George Washington Bridge to neighboring New Jersey to visit family, on a shopping trip to nearby White Plains. One day we received a nice present from relatives. Ability to purchase a brand new car of our own, and then hopefully drive out West. We did buy a Studebaker. It was a softish orange hued new car. I often later referred to it as our canned cream of tomato soup automobile. And when a deserved summer break got our out West yearnings too strong to resist, we two did set out in our brand new Studebaker to cross the country. The northern part of the country. We took along some sleeping bags so we could camp out now and then once we passed the urbanized area in our East. I have to just stop writing now, because I can easily picture all the interesting and scenic and historically revealing places that our new Studebaker headed to and left from and then new places headed to, and so forth, until we hit the Pacific Ocean facing part of our country.

As we two headed out west, there were smaller villages more interspersed between fields, little hills, heavily forested acres and acres, and it was a revealing contrast to the urban scene I was used to. Even when I lived upstate where buildings were less crowded together and where I could walk along the shores of beautiful Lake Cayuga and where there were frozen small waterfalls that eventually gushed water where we students could swim in the Spring and Summer, the sparseness of our country as we two headed further and further out West was striking. We could drive in our rear wheel drive cream of tomato soup colored stick shift car for over a day, until we ran out of the twenty-two cents per gallon gas, with only nature outside the windows. We sometimes purposely had to look for a so-called city to fill up on the gas again. Usually we found some cozy campsite to pull out the sleeping bags and take our rest. Sometimes we had to use the kind of motels that were typical of the area, small family run places with inexpensive rooms and free coffee and sugary donuts for early breakfasts. Then headed out west again. After camping at the shores of Lake Michigan, we got up early enough to catch the boat that carried us and our Studebaker for hours at early down, to the brightly lit up shore of Wisconsin.

We were not eager to hang around the urbanized city there but headed a bit southerly and further westward, where old forts and small towns with settler history dotted our way. The car radio was great for telling us about the local small town news and about the kind of humid or dry or sprinkly or non-weather we would come through for days upon days, for miles upon miles, where we resorted to stored up sandwiches and milk to light our way in the uninhabited jungles ahead. We did eventually come to a State called Oregon, and could see the vast tumbling waters of the Pacific Ocean. In fact we could not stop seeing these waters, because the highway going south to San Francisco was curving precariously atop some dunes that shielded humanity from the vast tumbling waters of that ocean. It was the kind of unforgettable drive where I kept my eyes shut most of the time while he insisted it was easy as he was used to driving since he was sixteen. The California roads were not the smooth multi-lane highways we had when I was growing up in the tri-state area. He was from that vast place called California and enjoyed returning to the bumpy dirt roads and an oncoming car or truck along that same slender curve did not at all phase him. I could hear the screeches and feel the sudden plop on the brakes, but mostly my eyes had to stay tightly shut. Not my mouth however, once we merged to better roads coming into that gold rush city of San Fran. All new to me. All new to my new Studebaker, which by now was covered with dust. Even the lush seats inside were revealing where we had been in the past days. Pieces of evergreen branches, little rocks from the shores of Lake Michigan, pieces of stamped boat tickets, some popsicle sticks and crushed milk cartons. By now there were lots of welcoming gas stations and we could stop, fill up, relieve ourselves, and try to sweep out some of the debris. I didn't need the sweaters and jackets from our camping days, and only wore a neat summery looking pale green matching blouse and pants, and probably some muddy encased sneakers. Soon we did meet up with his family and I got to ride the San Fran trolley, a reminder of my childhood days in Newark where we had criss-crossing trolleys all over our big flat city. This one was a Hemingway trolley car, high up and fast down Mount Kilimanjaroo, or so it felt to me.

We did continue south in the Studebaker along with his parents and had no need of the car radio as conversation was filling the air waves and I had every point of interest along the way displayed fluently to me. Even stopped for some formerly unknown food called enchiladas, and tacos, and there were Spanish, guess Mexican, speaking people helping out in the gas stations and restaurants and the colorful stands along the way.

Turns out that we eventually had to have our shiny, cleaned up inside and out Studebaker shipped back to New York for us, while we two used American Airlines to fly us home.

At home we soon moved above Manhattan to Westchester County, to garden apartments overlooking the Hudson River in Irvington-on-Hudson, and we had two little children there, both boys, who toddled and then skipped around the garden apartment campus with other young kids, and when we had to go to Manhattan to museums or to shop, we boarded the now infamous Hudson Rail Line, from Tarrytown to NYC. We kept our returned Studebaker which was so useful in all the shopping and sightseeing we did for a couple of years. End of that car story.

At our house nearby in Hastings-on-Hudson we by then had a Vauxhall, a more square shaped small car, which was bought at a Tarrytown dealer. Still a stick shift and I was driving my kids and myself around there for years. Elementary school days loomed and sleep-overs at their friends homes, and visiting family in New Jersey, all happened with this trusty little grey colored Vauxhall. Until one day we realized that for one year we would be living abroad, in Paris, France, where he had a physics job in a lab. No more Vauxhall, some nice friends took it off our hands for a few bucks.

We four sailed across the ocean, the Atlantic Ocean, on a big ship, took the French accented train to the big city with the French accent and totally strange food habits, and proceeded to acquire, as all Americans abroad did, a new car indeed. This was a beige colored Peugeot. It was very comfortable, lots of room for the boys and their trappings, and we used it perpetually, all over Paris, visiting charming French landmarks on week-ends, and then when the lab job was finished, traveling in our beige colored Peugeot south to see much more of this beautiful country. I am sighing again. So many visions crowd my mind. I must stop.

We did not confine this beige Peugeot to only its country of origin. We then drove north of that country, up to Belgium and Holland and all four of us had wonderful new sightseeing and wonderful new eating experiences thanks to the four wheeled vehicle. We were actually breaking it in for another bigger journey and its new life. We went back to America on a big ship and meanwhile the beige Peugeot, now defined as a used car, was shipped somehow over to Ellis Island. It passed the citizenship tests which were prevalent way back then, and shortly after we four people settled back home, we were able to bring our French vehicle to our own driveway and park it in our own garage. This was not original with us, as I mentioned, because travelers frequently did this to save some kind of money and have a nice car that could speak two languages easily. Admittedly it was not always easy to find a mechanic nearby once at home, who could attend to this foreign car, but once found, this mechanic was constantly patronized. Using the Peugeot also became a nice topic of conversation with strangers, much like walking your dog and then meeting friendly folk.

It was just an inanimate object, so we tried not to cry when we decided to trade it in and get a car that soon became the car of my dreams. It was a brown Mercury Cougar, low to the ground, easy for me to steer, and acceptable even in New Jersey where we moved for a year and bought it at a dealer there. Guess that is why it was so acceptable there. But all kidding aside, I loved driving this car, and enjoyed shifting with more stages, as drive, reverse, slow, fast, a brain challenge, and by now my two sons were in older grades and I could take them all over easily. One summer we spent out on Long Island where the father had a lab assignment, and with my treasured brown Mercury Cougar I drove my sons each day to go swimming at the ocean nearby. The Atlantic Ocean. A few years of believing that this low down smooth riding Cougar was more than just an inanimate object, and then all hell broke loose. One of our sons got taller and much more long legged suddenly and could not fit in the back seat anymore. Due to this bright and tall son, as usual, we had to change our way of life. Even though this trusty Cougar already had an adorable third baby son who could share the seats with the appropriate children car seats, belts, and so forth. Goodbye beautiful Cougar, and hello to the rapidly growing up wonderful family of three boys.

I am getting somewhat dizzy by now in trying to recall the makes and models and features of the next few cars that entered our lives. It was always the males in the family who went shopping for cars and they brought back stuff that pleased them. I was busy enough with gardening, getting music teachers for the sons, preparing larger and tastier meals for all those active guys. Rear drives started becoming front wheel drives and then four wheel drives, and the windows were supposed to open and close automatically by pressing buttons, although the buttons did not always work and there were family debates about who wanted more or less of the cold or the hot air to come in and over which door, and so I retreated to reading more and more books, which I loved to do, and when taking the literary sons to the local library often, I went through all the authors, from A to Z, each week. Discovered some new writers that way, when fiction books were on the main floor and before everything became digitized. I did not yet have a computer. But lots of different kinds of cars over the years, and there were favorite dealers who everyone knew, and so it went.

The memories of the first blue used Dodge hand me down covered truck that I had when driving up to college near Lake Cayuga are still strong and passionate. So many friends and such family background took place within and with that Dodge. Then the first Studebaker that was the color of canned cream of tomato soup and which drove the two of us all the way across this varied terrain and varied populated country to then look down upon the surging Pacific Ocean waves and soon shut my eyes as it tore along the narrow, high up curvy road to California, this is a never to be forgotten time. Gradually the cars spoke more languages, watched more growing up of children, changed technically, and it cost more and more to buy the gas. Not the original twenty-two cents a gallon like the olden days of yore. The car stories blended in with the trolley car and bus and subway and new tunnels and bridges stories, and left huge gaps in the stories when items like the Third Avenue high up L disappeared, except in paintings of its life.

(See Edward Hopper's painting)

Conclusion is that Cars Can Talk. And that Ladies Can Talk. Talk a Lot.

Gone But Remembered

So many beloved family members and friends are now gone, or were gone many, many ages ago, but are often remembered. This is not unusual for everybody, as passing away of elders and some peers is not inevitable. Constant reminders from the media also dwell on the images and lives of many passed away and deemed important figures. As expected.

However I find it most tragic that so many beautifully written books by heretofore very rightfully famous authors are now gone. I remember. But my local library seems to have an extremely short memory. Edwin Way Teale was a famous naturalist and entymologist, who wrote many, many books. He and his wife lived in a woodland surrounded cottage in Connecticut, which can still be visited, I am told. He also lived in New York City while attending the well known Columbia University, and he earned his MA degree there. Teale traveled thousands of miles across our country, taking back roads, not major highways which were not very prevalent anyhow at that time, and observed the trees, the plants, the birds, the other animals, the effects of the wind, the sun, the heat, the distance from the equator and the distance from the North Pole. His books were full of beautiful photographs and illustration and descriptions of what he observed. He won prizes and served as head of many nature societies. He was a most valued American author and his books were on the shelves of many people and on the shelves of many libraries, at the turn of the century. The forgotten nineteenth century.

He was in the process of writing a series of books about the seasons and when it came to writing about going North with the Spring, a tragedy hit him, more devastating than any wind, storm, tornado, or hurricane downed tree. He was informed of the death of their only son, David, who was serving in the armed forces during World War Two. Teale did write the book which was tempered by this tragedy in his life.

I recently looked up the author, Edwin Way Teale, in the digital, no longer card, catalog of my local library. How simplistic of me, a Senior Senior person, to expect the long list of his books. I worried that I would not know which of the many books to borrow first from my library. However, there was absolutely nothing by or about Edwin Way Teale in the digital catalog. I tried spelling different ways, and noting subject matter different ways. Now I will go physically into my local library and ask at the helpful desk there. Maybe it is just an oversight and they do really have at least a few of his books. Or else they can get them from another more complete neighboring library in our county or in our state or in our country.

When I do visit my local library I see reams of new books aligned on the shelves when one enters. Most are important books about how to cook vegetarian, how to broil a scallop, how to tell your boss that he is discriminatory, how to find a place for your petunia plants, and another large illustrated new book about how to find a place for your chrysanthemum plants, and also there are new biographies of important people who are actresses, TV personalities, Hippie composers and Rock stars, popular political characters, and admittedly one or two about well known anyhow composers, like Mozart. Since the shelves are overloaded in this manner, where could they possibly fit in any old book by a famous naturalist, let alone a new book with a carefully annotated biography of Teale.

Things certainly have changed over the past decades. Years ago I enjoyed reading novels and short stories in the numerous books that filled most of the main floor of this library. Now the fiction books have been delegated to the back of the floor below. On the main floor, and also in most of the space on the floor below, there are many computer "stations" where people can sit and look up what to read and sit and do their e-mail messages and try out many new web-sites. There are numerous shelves on the floor below stacked with DVDs and with CDs, and the library has a way of also listing these possibilities in its digital catalog.

For older folk and for newly arrived in our country folk, a couple of hours were set aside on the lower floor, once a week, to help us get assistance in using the computers we were struggling with. A library person was there to help us. Not any more. No, no, no. This service no longer exists. Instead the local library gives some courses which one has to register for, about using a Nook, and another about using an Ipad, and all those mobile devices that keep popping up in our stores, and of course, to purchase easily, with your credit card in hand, from sitting at home and ordering "on line".

I am perseverating and it is excusable to do so since I am classified as an "over 50" person. I am over 50, and I am over 60, and I am over 70, and only mid-80s. Maybe once I become "over 90" my question will be answered, but by then it will not matter to me, because my hand-eye coordination will be gone, and my cerebral left to right and right to left lobes will not work easily anymore. Perhaps some much younger individual might profit from an explanation from my architecturally expanded beautiful local library.

Where can I find a book, any book, by the famous naturalist named:

afterward: my library did manage to find a very well worn out book by Teale from a neighboring library in our town and I was allowed to borrow it for ten days, but I only gingerly turned its yellowed pages for fear of damaging them.

Hostas and Dogs and Chilliness
Milicent Tycko

By now it is early evening in the chilly Fall, and nothing better than to sit in dim light reading, with the still and fluffy and quietly breathing dog spread relaxed and warm on the sleeping bag that has become her winter bed spread inside out to accommodate her length and breadth. No hint at all about the afternoon outside in the big yard, when the hesitant and low lying sun condescended to briefly flash light on some of the flowers that were left after their summer expansions. A clump of pale pink chrysanthemums grasped the sunlight and featured themselves amidst the dark green shadowed tree trunks and leaves of almost invisible neighboring plants. Quickly the pink was side-stepped and then a swath of bright green lawn emerged in light surprisingly.

I stood up to let the brilliant green fill my eyes and then looked over the rail to see my hostas. Their huge leaves drooping slightly and miraculously changed from green to variegated yellow. A sure sign that their generous life all summer in producing tall stalks of purplish flowers was over. In dying this Fall day their waving broad leaves screamed out yellow to the world. My dog ran over and sniffed at them and then raced in floating manner up the little hill to hide herself amongst the other bushes.

I know the Fall colored hostas are waiting silently for next month's snow to cover them up. All that is left in color then will be the clump of pale pink chrysanthemums and the surrounding swaying trees almost bereft of their briefly colored Fall leaves.

In early evening she is with me again... Her doggie meals will be eaten quickly, her water will be lapped up happily, and she will lie near our kitchen table while we humans have our dinner. When I go to the other room and switch on the TV, she will come along also and lie close with her head getting scratched and her legs getting massaged and her belly getting scratched. Then she will distance herself and seemingly be fast asleep. But when I finally do go to the bedroom she will quickly come along without being asked and curl up happily on the sleeping bag.. The sleeping bag is also covered for added thickness with a woolen blanket, so chilly nights will be easy to take.

The brilliant yellow hosta leaves come along with me as I close my eyes to sleep and I am so happy to see this in my mind while my dog lies quietly nearby. I know that she is having her dog dreams when her legs seem to twitch as if running fast and she makes a small yelp. She is guardian through the night. If a car motor is heard a few blocks away she will rise up and bark and if she is told that it is okay, then she will return to her dog dreams.

In the morning she is in no hurry to get going in the Fall. She follows with her eyes as I get bathed and dressed but makes no move. Then when I say that it is UP time, she stretches and comes to lick my hand and we go back through the kitchen to put on the little leash.. Outdoors, she checks out the overnight smells left by squirrels and birds, then dashes like a feather blown by fierce winds up the hill, around the fence, down the garden paths and around and around the yard. At breakfast time she will be lying outside on the dew damped grass just looking around, until she gets her biscuits and kibbles..

Tomorrow I hope to go outdoors and call my dog and gaze over the garden looking for the limp yellow hosta leaves and the pink chrysanthemum clump. It will be hard at first, because the Fall sun is very loathe to gain altitude, and wants to creep very slowly toward its afternoon radiance. Will my hostas still be yellow or just down on the earth by then?

I know my dog will jump about and run towards and away and towards and away all day until it is evening and time for dinner, TV, bed, and hosta dreams..

Today's Outing With Our Dog

Our border collie was jumping for joy this morning when we told her she could come along for a ride in our car. She hates waiting at home alone, even if we are away for a short while doing chores. Princess behaves well in the back seat of our Suburu truck and I have a couple of pillows for her to lie on. Once we park at the village Post Office, of course she tries to get out the door. But only one of us took the letters to mail, so she had company in the car while waiting. A nice older gentlemen noticed her and came over to just say hello and maybe pat her through the partially open window. At first she kind of gave his hand a lick, but as soon as he started to chat, my dog barked and barked as if saying: Hey, guy, I am here to protect my lady, and you have just crossed the border. Scram away. He bent back and said Okay. You are protecting. I understand.

When the driver came back carrying a package of received letters, then Princess wagged her tail and sat back down as usual. So I suggested we drive over to the big area parking lot, surrounded by a forest of trees, and take her out for her familiar walk there. Which we did. She leapt out the truck door and I told her to wait a minute while I got her long leash firmly in hand. Then hubby also got out, and we followed her while she explored the plants and the soil and politely used the rest rooms she knew by heart along the plants surrounding the lot. A few cars were parked here and there. At the farthest end of this lot, there was a big red truck parked next to a smaller white car. It was the man whose truck it was, we discovered, who was also walking around the circle lot, meanwhile talking into his hand held device. He seemed to have a lot to say and a lot to listen to. As long as he kept his distance, we walked with our dog back and forth, along the forest like edge of the lot, pausing for her to investigate the spots she liked. If I told her Okay, now we go back, she readily turned to go the other way.

The red truck guy, being so engrossed in his conversation with his hand, obviously did not notice us, and crossed too near, and Princess then pulled hard on the lease and barked and leapt. This was her territory, was it not? The guy reared away once he woke up to reality, and we pulled our dog back. So it was okay. It was after this interlude on the lot that I noticed that that guy went to the red truck and got into it. So that is who he was. The driver of the red truck, which stayed parked at the farthest end of the lot, next to the white car. We continued our slow circling happily, and if it was up to Princess, she could spend hours there. It was hilly in the area above the lot and lots of fallen branches, unusual vegetation, washed down mud, to explore.

By now we felt it would be time to get back into our dented grey Suburu, and so reluctantly the dog was urged to jump in, and so did we two. Meanwhile I glanced again at those two parked vehicles at the far end of the lot, and was surprised to see the passenger door of the truck open slowly, and two legs, with lady shoes and tight slacks on, emerged, as did the rest of the casually dressed young lady. She had appropriate sporty casual jacket on, and remained chatting for a while with the red truck driver. Then it finally concluded, and she opened her next door white car and got into her own driver's seat. Both vehicles stayed there as if glued to the road, so we started driving off. Then slowly the red truck did back around. I said to wait until he got the hell out of there, and we never did find out about the lady in the white car, which stayed. We drove away. Then we parked our grey dented truck with the dog reluctantly having to remain seated in it, left the windows slightly open, and got out to walk to our favorite deli store there and have a caloric snack or two.

My Sicilian pizza, large corner slice, was delicious, and my husband's chicken and cheese in toasted roll was being eaten with relish. But, being of the talkative gender, I mused out loud. Isn't it strange that that red truck and the car and then those two were parked so far from the rest of the busy shops, and stayed so long, and he getting instructions on his hand, and then finally the duo could split? Was it a supposedly surreptitious drug deal? Which sure had the appearance. An exchange of sorts, between two innocent looking dealers at the edge of a nice middle-class village?

Or was it an off the record romance, extra marital for him, or was it a paid performance? So strange, and my thick pizza with gooey cheese and tomato sauce was so good also

Let us be nice, and make up a very nice explanation. The girl is his niece and he is arranging with another cousin of hers, as to where and what time, he should tell his niece to go meet the cousin. Or was he finding a possible cashier job for his daughter and calling his business friend on his hand device to see of an opening.

Meanwhile, the deli food was disappearing rapidly, and I suggested we save some to take home and finish up later in the day, which we did. By now it was overdue to get back in the dented grey Suburu and say hello again to our impatient border collie, and promise that now we go home, home, home Princess. All was normal and we did get back in our own garage a few blocks from the village with a pile of new letters, mostly bills to read, and a tempting bag of Italian goodies to carry up to the kitchen table. So, that is our outing with our dog for today.

Loss of our Basset Tippy

(Our First Doggie)

Our 12-year-old lovable basset-hound Tippette (Tippy) did not make it through this extra-cold winter, and after a week of bad cough developed pneumonia. Being retired Seniors, my husband and I had become bonded inextricably to her. She was always with us, whether camping in New England, at the seashore on Long Island where we live, and even on our cross-country driving trip to Bellingham, Washington, where we boarded the Inner Passage Ferry with Tippy along, to have a scenic trip. She made friends for us wherever we went, as people stopped to pat her, and she always looked for an audience and gave us the chance to talk to people from all walks of life. Our little grandkids adored her.

When she was put to sleep in kindly manner, we had her buried in the Pet Cemetery here on Long Island, and attended her funeral there with aching hearts. A beautiful pinkish colored stone monument was made for her by a sympathetic workman, whose understanding of our grief was some comfort. We have gone to visit her there every few weeks and plant some perennials, like primroses, a small hedge, recently some grape hyacinths, in order to have a sequence of colors, all within a small triangle with a little green fence around. It is a comfort that there are other much loved pets all around her. We think to ourselves that this is such a peaceful place and full of love, because all the pets (dogs, cats, horses, birds) laid to rest there must have been dearly loved and returned torrents of love to their owners. This might be in contrast to the cemeteries where we humans bury family members, who in the course of their average human lives certainly did have some unlovable and maybe even hostile traits. Not so with the pets. Love abounds, as it did last weekend when the shaft of sun through the surrounding trees highlighted Tippy's pinkish marble headstone and where a flock of birds suddenly swooped down across that shaft of sun, like an air honor guard, to tell us that nature was always protecting her spirit.

Our feelings over the recent loss of our pet.

Our brick enclosed fireplace

"Camping Out"
Camping in with
my home fireplace
By
MG. T

Camping Out

Tall sputtering orange flames in my winter fireplace acted almost as glue in fixating my vision. The variety of woods and papers were creating short blue and medium tall yellow leaps of hot fire which sprung up rapidly from the iron grate. The intermittent sputtering and crackling sounds were a sound and light symphony and I settled back in my old armchair. The look of this nightly beauty which we accompanied by sitting and finishing our last cup of dinner coffee relaxed my face and my cataract corrected eyes closed slowly from time to time. The glowing red embers grew higher under the iron grate in the brick fireplace and became too bright for my eyes. I had become elderly and was grateful that we could sit in comfort by our fireplace. It all led to a trail of old images from years and decades ago when we two had also enjoyed the leaping flames and glowing embers with no need to rely on our indoor fireplace in our little ranch house on Long Island where we have lived for over four decades.

We used to be camping out. We used to enthusiastically go camping out. We used to pull our small camper behind our small truck and head out East. We used to find almost empty campsites out East on Long Island when we headed there, often with our dog in tow, because we were savvy back then. We knew that if we rumble on in the opposite direction from those driving back towards work and towards the city, then our roaring ocean and our full high sky would not have to be interfered with by noisy loud radios and screaming kids all night long. Only us older folk would be there and we were all wise enough to grab the sites that had spaces in between. We could chose whether we wanted to be near the rising tide so we could wade out soon in the morning or late at night or whether we wanted to be closer to the road so we could quickly drive our little truck out once our camper was settled and go looking for small grocery stores to get supplies or go looking for the beaches that were ready for fishermen or go looking for the little thrift shops in the nearby quaint villages so we could go antique fishing. It was glorious and we always gathered up left over wood from the other abandoned campsites and roamed the beach fronts for old drifted up wood amidst the cans and bottles left by weekenders and our dog could run and sniff and get her paws wet a low tide.

Our campsite was quickly loaded up with burnables and we had a large stack of gathered up wood to feed the large iron outdoor burners on the ground next to our camper. The crackling of this outdoor fire was surrounded by the fluttering wings and caw caws of the overhead spinning around birds and the pulsating rhythm of the ocean waves. The high tide coming in was especially musical as it slowly crescendoed just as our grilled hamburgers were getting ready to eat and if we stayed long enough in the darkening hours while the flames were still being fed by smaller sticks and wads of cardboard we could toast up our marshmallows as the tide slowly receded and the sound of the waves diminished. All this was music for our lives and we knew that other people were humming along quietly or whispering softly to each other as they also enjoyed the spacious campgrounds near the sea.

The beauty of being out East where there were so many places to gather up assorted colored shells and pebbles and rocks is that when our wandering instinct needed more and more wandering to be satisfied, we could conveniently find a ferry boat nearby which liked to carry campers and their burdens of canvas tents and small and large pop-up campers and Rvs.

Those ferry rides with all the other barking dogs and chattering people filled with the expectation of soon rumbling down the gangplank to another island were fun to remember. Bumping along new unpaved roads and seeing rocky hills and then mysterious enclaves with hidden dunes and sudden splashing waves that came from France or Belgium or England across the Atlantic sea was thrilling. Our beloved Long Island seemed to have many beautiful and yet strangely different smaller relatives nearby. Our beloved long and mainly flat Long Island reached out eastward with arms of sand and rock and seaweed to other mountain and valley covered nearby islands where we could land and camp and then leave in rhythm just as the fish and crabs and shells did. We could discover new places and loads of burnable old branch bark and old sea-torn wads of paper from the old pirate ships that were now strewn on these nearby shores and we could make our leaping flames and warm our toes near colorful fires that no person had manufactured an iron grate for and never would.

My fluttering eyelids once more opened wide to see our brick ensconced fireplace again and to see that it was crying out for more wood to burn. We did not have to comb the beach for wood. We only had to reach down to our neatly stacked pile of trimmed to size branches and logs. The flames cried out gratefully as new wood was added onto the iron grate and a display of tall yellow and orange and small blue flames again danced safely in the fireplace. A couple of tin foil wrapped sweet potatoes sat peacefully amongst the glowing hot red embers below. If my eyelids driftily closed again I could relish the charcoal coated hamburgers and the browned marshmallows from our camping out days and years on our beloved Eastern Long Island. I could even smell the toasted pieces of recently caught fresh fish that we put onto our outdoor campfires as they dripped juicily and sputtered sparks of fish scales onto the sand around. My eyelids were pulled open by the aroma of this memory and then I could stare with wonder at our indoor fireplace.

The long island we still lived on was by now almost overgrown with many new houses and roads but would always be there to reach the sea and be cooled and warmed and brow - beaten by the sea and always persist in offering calm days with softly rippling tides that beckoned young feet to wade. The East end would grow and recede and grow out again over more and more decades. The places to park campers would always be there for the little screened canvas pop-ups as well as the big snoring metal six or eight wheel recreational vehicles. The fancy folk would spin shiny cars from the city towards the sandy dunes out east and the hoards of plebian folk would crank their dented cars out to the end. They would all enjoy splashing in their swimsuits in summer and walking the isolated strands in their mufflers and woolen cardigans in winter. Their dogs would freely run about the colorful and multi patterned rocks and the squashed old bottles and cans and the washed ashore branches and old cartons. The lonely fishermen in their rubber boots and warm coats with hoods would always be there aiming their rods far out in the ocean. Then they would come home and remember those times as they warmed themselves in front of their brick fireplaces in their houses in wintertime and in their own personal old age wintertime.

I rose from padded chair that snuggled me as our dancing flames displayed their banners on the iron grate within our fireplace now. I sought my nearby desk and the stacks of stapled papers upon which I had written so many impressions over the years. I knew that much of this was created in our little canvas pop-up when we sat within waiting for the rain to let up. Or when he was out fishing in the early morning and I was scrawling words on old menus while I cooked up something for our breakfasts. Or as I sat with a small pad in hand upon the old blanket on the sand and watched our children stay close enough as they practiced swimming and ran back to the blanket for their sandwiches and chocolate cookies and towels. Many meditative words poured out and finding them again did amuse my moments of recollection. I thumbed through these papers and realized that they all owed their creation to the days I was camping out on the East end of Long Island.

Safely alone in the evening near to our campsite I had practiced my yoga once and wrote of Yoga at the Sea:

> I sit on the ocean front sand
> With legs crossed in my yoga pose
> Careful to take no space on the thin yellow strand
> Which soon darkens until
> I reflect on the moonscape
> Merged seamlessly still
> With the seascape
> Absorbing me placidly
>
> All of my thoughts remain
> Focused, as taught,
> On my rhythm of breathing
> My rhythm of slowness
> Legato andante
> Held steady for hours
> As I watched the

Merged moonscape
Dissolve in the sea
And awakening light
Dimly peer before sun
Made the ripples of sea
Become evident telling me
Time was well spent
Rising up I depart

I was not alone then but rather surrounded by the seagulls and waves and knowing that nearby was our quiet and safe campsite on the beautiful East end facing the ocean.

The changing ocean fed into a salty lake nearby in Montauk where we both sat enjoying the autumnal quiet now that the tourists had left to return to work and to school.

My indoor brick fireplace at home was winding down its sound and light displays and so I was reminded of our stay at Montauk harbor where I wrote these words back in 1991:

The brick encased fireplace was by now holding only a few glowing small branches and the underlying embers were piled high and slowly becoming more dim. The coffee cups had long been emptied. This meant that it was time for bed in a mood made happy by my memories of camping out on the East end of my beloved and very long and mainly flat Long Island.

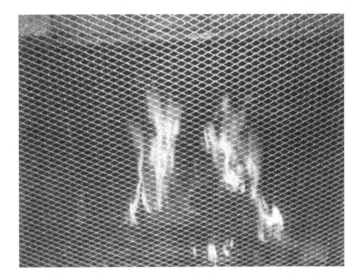

"Camping Out"
Then "Camping In" with
my home
fireplace
MGT

Sparrows And Puppies

Some love sparrows more than anything else in this world. Some love puppies more than anything else in this world. This defines two persons very succinctly. If there happens to be a sparrow sitting on the rail of the porch outdoors, then in a split second he will notice and talk about this sparrow. Even if he has to stop eating for that moment. If there is a doggie walking by, a young puppy or a large dog, she will immediately smile and go outdoors, if not already outdoors and wave to that doggie. Her own doggie will alert her by immediately running around and around the backyard, quicker than any greyhound or any race horse. And her own doggie might have just been lying quietly on the back deck before taking off rapidly.

It is not that the sparrow lover only goes for sparrows. He is quite fond of their doggie, and will often notice other doggies while out for a walk. It is not that the puppy lover does not enjoy seeing and hearing birds. Though she is usually more impressed by the cardinals and morning doves. There are so many, many sparrows in their yard, on the roof, flying all over the high trees on their property, and sometimes in a big flock, but sometimes only one or maybe two sparrows at first.

There are reasons for these obvious preferences. Historical reasons. Personal reasons. Family background reasons. Just as it is necessary to wait with patience for a sighting of the morning doves, it is necessary to have patience in learning about the reasons which lurk behind the preferences for either Sparrows or Puppies.

If as a young child, growing up very, very gradually in Los Angeles, one had a grandma and grandpa who had a chicken and egg farm, when surrounding areas very rural, and you stayed with them on their flourishing chicken and egg farm for the summer, then you certainly

39

had lots of chicken and egg experiences. He often talked to her, even now when they were in their mid-eighties, about his summers with grandma and grandpa on their rural farm, which supplied locals with their eggs and chickens and on holidays, with their turkeys. It does sound like a lot of fun. He would run freely around the acres, and he was given the jobs of collecting some eggs from the chicken coops, without breaking them. Without breaking the eggs, no matter about the coops. He also could help his mechanically apt grandpa put together new chicken coops, using nice clean wooden planks. He could hold up the plank at the right angle while grandpa nailed it in place. In those bygone days there were no plastic chicken coops to buy easily, no factories making anything, as it was well before World War Two, when a rapid metamorphosis occurred in Los Angeles due to thousands of people flooding that area to make airplanes and bombs to fight the Nazis, to fight the Japs, and big ships had to be outfitted to haul soldiers and sailors, drafted young boys, across the Pacific Ocean to fight.

No, it was a quiet time, with loads of big stretches of rural land surrounding the low population of Los Angeles in that era.

So, he enjoyed helping Grandpa put together his own clean wooden plank coops. Mainly he enjoyed collecting eggs, without breaking them. He loved watching his Grandma pluck the feathers from a chicken and then taking it into her big old-fashioned kitchen to prepare for dinner. Yummy, what a great cook was Grandma. No servants to help lift the pots to the oven, to help slicing the home grown onions and green peppers, to help splash a home-made marinade over the soon to be roasted and then very quickly taken out of the oven, sliced up somewhat, and served on a big platter to hard working Grandpa, and to that hungry child who helped collect eggs. These were ways of preparing and cooking that came down for hundreds of years to his Grandma and Grandpa, who had recently come over from the old country. Whose ancestors preserved every tiny bit of food, never wasting a scrap, because they were in little shtetls and did not have easy access to shops. Out of the question even today, for a grand big SuperMarket. All this kept them in business, selling to the locals. They even raised turkeys as a special treat for the American feast of Thanksgiving, a new one that the old country folk happily learned about.

Of course Grandma made her own stuffings for the birds, using her creative brain each time, no books of recipes to read, no preordained stuffing mixes to buy in a SuperMarket either. If bread was needed, then her own baked bread a few days old, was crumbled up and became the key part of her stuffings. After the chickens were roasted, all the fat that had dripped from them, was collected and saved as Shmalz, to use later on freshly baked slices of bread. No bought package of White Bread in cellophane wrappers, no Margarine, heaven forbid.

Easy to understand that his sparrow loving inclinations had evolved from his personal family background, tending to the chickens and eggs with beloved Grandma and Grandpa.

Not the only thing. Also, in the backyard of his parents' home he had a gift given to him, of a duck. Snowy white duck. So named, with an original twist: SNOWY. That duck raised its own family in that yard and was a constant source of interest for him. She, the puppy lover who now shared many decades of togetherness with him, was never ever spared for more than 2 weeks hearing more about his beloved SNOWY. She did have beloved puppies and dogs in her own life, but kept it kind of quiet. More on this topic, on her topic, later on. That is why patience is required of any reader of Sparrows and Puppies.

He also raised pigeons as did some of his boyhood friends. Before the Internet, pigeons were valued for flying over with messages and always returning home with replies.

Now their large backyard, where the kitchen, smaller by far than his beloved Grandma's kitchen, luckily had windows facing out side, where the small deck was. The deck recently painted light brown, with railings around it and a little gate with two steps down to the big backyard. At last we are allowed to focus on something in the title of this gruesomely long story. A SPARROW alighted on to the deck railing and just sat there, peering into the kitchen where he and she sat at their little maple table eating their healthy breakfast. A big clink-clunk. She knew by now what caused his spoon to drop onto the maple table. He saw his sparrow sitting on the deck railing with tiny eyes peering in. Okay. I know you are there. I know you are unbearably hungry for your bird seeds. So he retrieved the spoon, quickly gulped down the rest of his healthy cooked oatmeal, and went out the back door. He was chatting a lot to the sparrow, as he walked down the two steps, with the jar of assorted bird seeds, over to the wooden feeder that rested on a stool a few yards away from the back deck and screen house on the back deck. Here you go, and he was chatting and mumbling to the sparrow, who by now was with many of her relatives, all flying down fast from surrounding trees and bushes, and hopping onto the wooden bird feeder. He had made this square wooden feeder a few years ago from clean, fresh wood. Having learned how to make coops from his beloved Grandpa years ago, over seventy-five years ago, it came easily for him to put together this little wooden feeder which sat on the stool. Then he walked across the back lawn, meanwhile noticing how the various plants were blooming, or about to bloom, or by now shedding spent leaves.

When he got up on the deck, she had already finished her little dish of oatmeal, and brought outdoors two cups of coffee to place on the table in the screenhouse. This was the routine. Then they both could sit down and watch all the different birds at the feeder, meanwhile slowly sipping their coffee. Hers had almond milk in it, his was his preferred black. They did like coffee a lot, having evolved in a couple of generations from their great-great or great-great-great grandparents who only drank tea in their old countries. Only now, in America, was coffee available, and even so, just their plain old grandparents preferred tea, sometimes sipping it from a saucer with a lump of sugar between their teeth. Ah, the olden days of yore

She did enjoy seeing the various birds, but due to some hearing diminishment, she did not usually hear their songs and calls. He alerted her to them. She was frankly bored with all the various "sparrows", the long tailed ones, the blackish ones, the usual brown ones, the more unusual brown ones with sharp white streaks on sides of their little heads, even the ones that were greyish-brown with very creamy shaded white all over their bellies. She loved the red cardinals, and especially the slightly duller red lady cardinals. It was fun to watch Mr. Cardinal feeding, as if kissing, Mrs. Cardinal, as she grew more and more plumper before laying her cardinal egg in their nest. The bluejays looked colorful but she did not like to see them come down and chase all the other birds and then sit and rudely gobble up all the seeds they could. She mostly waited for the pair of greyish morning doves to gently fly over, sit patiently on the grass around the stool with the bird feeder box on it, and then alight and slowly nibble their food.

Sparrows were all birds to them, and all birds did fill their yards, back and front, with beautiful sounds and sights, from dawn to dusk. At night it was quiet except for an owl who did hoot from one of their trees. Who could not love birds? But not everyone tried to act like an Ornithology Professor from Cornell University, listening, sighting, naming from his bird book, as many as possible, and despairing when a certain bird resisted being catalogued. Not she. It was more relaxing for her, when it came to birds.

Not when it came to cooking. Lots of cooking and baking books. Made up her own bread recipes. Made up her own soups But even more was dogs. Not when it came to puppies and doggies. No, no, no. She had tons of dog books, descriptions of breeds, collections of dog stories. She was overly fond of almost all dogs, and especially now when she cared for and loved her adopted Border Collie named Princess. Always Princess, even when abused by former owner before she was rescued to the animal shelter. She kept the name Princess, because that was her name, and she could never marry and have to change her name, because she was already spayed. It was sad sometimes, as she knew that Princess would be overjoyed to mother some puppies. Not to be. But when she met with other dogs, or had dog visitors, she was as social and fluffy tail wagging as could be. Her cousin who loved this dog suggested she be named Queenie. But that was not her own name, and also was kind of mundane.

Before having Princess, who was almost 7 years old, they did have another dog, a Basset Hound which they named Tippette Fromage, because she loved cheese so much. This was not a rescued dog, but bought as a brand new puppy in a store that still was allowed to deal in dogs that were bred in other states and then sold. Although they had looked at other young Basset Hounds recently in other shops, this is the one that immediately caught their eyes. She was mainly white, with a few splotches of tan on her back and her ears were very, very long. They bought her on first sight and brought home an untrained adorable puppy. She spent her first few months biting and scratching the legs of their wooden chairs, and in the evenings one or the other of the people had to sleep on an armchair in the den where Tippy lay cozily on the couch nearby. Every couple of hours they woke her and took her outdoors to do her business. If it was a starry night it was okay, but sometimes it was raining or extremely dark and even so they did what had to be done. Gradually Tippette learned to never use the indoor floors or carpets to do her business, and so by a year or so, they had brought up a well behaved and beautiful long eared dog, with flat fur that did not require continual brushing all summer, as did the fur of her Princess. When Tippy died at 12 years, they cried a lot, but remembered how nice that they had gone camping with her, had even driven in their truck all the way across the country with her along and gone up by ferry to see part of Alaska with her on the boat, then home again.

Tippy lay on the floor of the truck quietly, sometimes she could sit up front in the passenger seat and help us steer the car.

We were resolved to not have any other dog, but before long could not resist the rescued Border Collie, who became so close to them.

Growing up the woman always had dogs, various kinds, in the home, where her parents treated the dogs just like their own two children. In those days dogs could just be let out the door without a leach, and roam around the neighborhoods. It was natural for them, and they could meet up with other doggie friends, and do activities together. They could also very easily mate and then come home to bring their puppies into the world, and only then could the owners guess who the daddies had been. If they had a male dog, then no matter. It was a patriarcle society for dogs.

She remembered Skippy, her young brother's favorite long white furred collie and so many photos showed her young brother, even dressed with a hat and jacket, sitting on the front steps of their house with Skippy next to him, being held tightly.

They had a chow dog, with gorgeous red fur, and the two kids would walk their chow, by then with a leash, around the block each day. But once, when the mailman, who delivered letters by hand to each of us back then, came up to our second floor apartment and opened the door, the chow lunged at the poor guy, and gave him an unpleasant bite. So, we did have to get rid of this gorgeous chow, which the authorities managed.

In later young adult life, when sister was busy going to college from home already, her younger brother had a dog, probably called Brownie, who was very musical. By then brother was an advanced trumpet player in the high school band, and he would sit in their living room and purposely go up and down the scale loudly and clearly with his shiny trumpet. And Brownie sat in front of him and howled with head up in the air, in synchrony. If there was a silent pause, then Brownie just sat down calmly and waited. Again the trumpet tones and the dog immediately howled in company with the trumpet.

Once grown up and married and living in their little suburban house, along with their own sons, he and she decided that their kids would like to have a doggie in their house to play with. So they got a nice medium sized tan dog, who was fun and the other kids in the neighborhood came over and played with the frisky dog in their yard where they also went swinging and sliding on the play gym. But, since hubby and I both went out to work by now, and had to leave the school age kids and their doggie with a child sitter, the dog did get out of hand, and unfortunately nipped one of their playful friends on the knee, not meaning harm but being part of the play party. Not acceptable of course to those kid's parents, and so the dog had to be returned to its shelter. We all prayed that doggie would find another friendly home.

So it went along and sons grew up and us parents of many years were alone in our house. We did have fish aquariums and some birds in cages now and then, as our youngest son was still home and not yet away in college. But not to always be so, and eventually we really felt an empty house, even with occasional guests and the TV shows and cooking and baking and other chores. So then we did succumb to buy our Tippy, a lovable Basset Hound who liked to eat cheese and who enjoyed camping and helping us drive the truck across the country and up on the ferry to Alaska. Had to put her down with bad case of pneumonia at 12 yrs.

That is it. No more dogs. Unendurable however. Met Princess eye to eye while casually visiting the Shelter out east, and could not resist. They said we were "too old to handle such an active Border Collie". We returned next week, and once again Princess stopped circling in her den, paused and looked at me eye to eye. I want to be yours. Please. So the management decided it was the only way they would find a decent home for such an active dog and agreed. Having a dog crate still in the back of the truck, we took her, she jumped up, and has been with us for almost seven happy years, keeping us active and young. She has made the home, the neighborhood, the local village and all along the shore of the nearby Long Island Sound, filled with happy waves. She also enjoys listening for the songs and calls of the birds and gazing at them and chasing away those annoying squirrels. Hooray. This story called Sparrows and Puppies has reached the end. You may add to this if you also enjoy Birds and Doggies. Please do.

Goldfish And Kittens

Now I must write a sequel to my story called: Sparrows and Puppies. Why must I do this. Because puppies and doggies are very adorable and have formed a very happy ongoing time in my very long life. From my childhood up until now, when I am in my mid – eighties. It was irresistible to recall all the puppies and doggies. However, it has become insistently necessary to tell myself that there is still a large, open space, unoccupied, in the long years of my life. The reminders keep coming to me, whether during the daytime or early nighttime, or upon waking up before dawn. What about me, meow the little kittens. Did you forget about me, meow the older pussy – cats. Why oh why do you neglect to talk about us, mourn all the cats, wailing and wailing.

I never ever forget you, all of you little helpless kittens and all of you large cats, the ones who only lived in the house, and the ones who were let outdoors to roam in the nighttime, and the ones who grew heavier and heavier while carrying their unborn kittens in their furry abdomens, and the ones who lay expectantly on their blanketed cat beds while he gently helped the tiny blind newborns get out of that big cat's abdomen, one by one. He placed each tiny kitten in a row near mommy cat, and sometimes it took many hours. Of course it started in the evening, after his dinner, and went on so long that he only could catch a few hours sleep for himself when over. He wanted to stay near to them and admire the scene and he could hardly wait to describe the ordeal to her and her sons once they awoke at the usual morning hour, in time for breakfast, dressing hurriedly for school, and for her, excitedly listening to him while washing up the dishes. She had to go watch over the mother cat and new babies.

So she never ever did neglect to think of the kittens and cats in her own life. In her life as a child. In her life as a supposedly grown up woman.

His staying up most of the night to help mother cat, called Mayfly, deliver her kittens, was actually not a new experience for him. He had a similar, but initial experience delivering kittens to our former cat named Ursula. That was over twelve years ago, and when morning came he could not tell the story to his sons because they were not yet born. None of them. Only some teensy weensy kittens were born that night. Narrating about the scene to her also had to be somewhat toned down, because she was also carrying a heavy abdomen with a soon to be born first baby inside. Not known yet if it was a boy or girl baby. But back in those less technical days before inter-uterine x, y, or z rays were done, at least they did know one fact for sure. It was definitely NOT a teensy weensy kitten. Not a teensy girl kitten or a teensy boy kitten. And it would probably take many years for their new baby to try walking and talking. It could not even Meow softly.

Now the reader is given a preview of Ursula and of Mayfly, both cats in my adult supposedly grown up years. Both cats in my married to the same him years. I named our first cat Ursula after an Ursula and Gudrun story, you know which one of course. I used to read this author a lot back then. Then when my first son was already over ten years old, and loved to go fishing when we lived on Long Island, he said to name the cat Mayfly, which is some kind of a fish lure. Named somehow after those annoying crowd of insects called Mayflys. How that kitten came to our house, is due to our third, youngest son who was shopping with me in the local Bohack market. Outside there were kids with a bunch of kittens in their cart. They were told, I guess, to give them away. And our young son wanted our Mayfly, a really pretty white and grey kitten. She grew up with him for over eighteen years, always sitting on his lap, and when he left for college and came home, the first thing he did was look for our Mayfly, who lived for over twenty years, and seldom wandered away from our yard, until her last forgetful few weeks. The other sons also liked her and fed her, but she really was almost a twin with our youngest boy. Learned to play together and she slept in his room.

Kittens started way back in my childhood however. The afore mentioned puppies and doggies were part of our family. Well, the same goes for the kittens and cats.

When I was a child of about eight or nine years old, we lived on the second floor of a two story house.

My most loved young cat was called by me: Faldeo I still treasure photos of me cuddling Faldeo in my arms. She jumped into my arms as soon as I came home from school. A couple of years of this. She was an indoor cat, and such fun to be feeding her the dish of milk, or leftover fish pieces from our dinners, or whatever crumbly stuff we could mix up with fish. Not with Goldfish, we never ate Goldfish. Just watched them swim in our little bowls of water.

How did it happen, I have suppressed it exactly. But one afternoon, while holding Fal-de-O in my arms at the top of the staircase, I must have tripped or tried to get something else, maybe a fallen book, with my other arm, but then carelessly dropped her and she plunged down the steps, rollin over a few at a time. My brother and I ran down to get her, but she was sorely wounded, and her legs all broken. So our parents said they had to take her someplace and have her "put down" because she suffered too much. I cried into my pillow for days, and to this exact moment I want her back and am talking to her. I think I named her Fal -de-O after a musical scale I learned, do-re-me-fa-sol,,,,,,,,,,,,,,,sing and dance in kitten heaven please, my Fal -de -O.

A few years after that, we had a one family house which had a basement and a "crawl space" under the front porch and steps. The very same steps upon which my younger brother sat with his beloved long haired furry collie dog named Skippy. We kids were free to go out and play, in the school yard, on the sidewalks, and were always running and playing all over the neighborhood with other kids and welcomed to go in and out of the other's houses. Here I was down in the basement of our house with two of my girlfriends when we heard a slight hushed sound that made us slowly look more into that crawl space under the front porch and steps. It was a terribly dusty and dark space. Not ever went there. But we were brave and could not resist putting our hands into that heap of grey dust which flew around. My G-D. There were a few moving objects. Those objects felt furry, which was not just the dusty film. Those objects started to quietly say meow, meow, meow. They were poor little newborn kittens, whose mother had been smart enough to find a safe and private place to lie down in and then let her kittens come out, one by one. We ran upstairs to announce the discovery to the parents, who rushed down with us and took those kittens out, one by one, and wrapped them in a soft blanket that they had brought along. Mommy cat trudged out also. Then that new cat family was given a kinder place to be, lying on the basement floor, near to the warm furnace on a few old blankets. Where they remained. We visited them daily with some milk and goodies, not chocolate-chip cookies, but old cans of partially eaten tuna fish or sardines. They grew up in a couple of weeks, so we opened the basement door and when they wanted to, they all ran outdoors. Now they had become what is now called Feral Cats, and good for them. Nobody bothered to "spay" them, so no doubt they populated our neighborhood for years to come.

Goldfish are so pretty, so dainty, and so bright yellow as they gently swim around. All that was needed to accommodate them was a small "goldfish bowl", which took up very little space on top of a bookcase, or as a centerpiece on the dining-room table. When one of our young granddaughters was a child, she did not have any pets in her house. Her parents did not care to have fur or hair or paw prints all over their new house. But being sympathetic grandparents, one day we brought over a gift, wrapped carefully in white tissue paper, of a bowl with a goldfish swimming in it. How could anyone resist? And our young granddaughter and her younger still brother, enjoyed watching the goldfish swim slowly in the water. They gave fresh water each day. When we visited them again, it was a happy scene and we even still have a photo of the children and their goldfish in the bowl. I say "still have" because the fish did pass on, and then the bowl was cleaned well, and stored away someplace. Maybe used as a flower vase in Spring.

The great big fish tank that later on became a feature in our den, was never ever intended to become a flower vase. Our youngest son picked out this tank at a store specializing in unusual tank fish. Not for fishing rods. Only for sitting on a big, strong shelf, with devices attached to keep the water bubbling constantly so oxygen circulated, and the fish could feel at home, as if really undersea. New fish were added each week when we went shopping. Who ever remembers all their names? It seems that Guppies were all over that tank. But of great use were the couple of dark fish that constantly ate algae off of the insides of the tank. They kept it very clean, and they grew quite heavy doing this. Of course then we had to purchase a little cave like structure to place inside on the bottom of the tank. Fish could swim in and out of the archways, or hide inside, and it looked so natural, like a real undersea coral structure. Books about fish accumulated near the tank also. Once when the house electricity went off due to a storm outdoors, all went dark in the tank, and it took a while for parents to realize what was going on. They tried to re-attach the wires, and probably lost some of the fish. Then it was deemed advisable to purchase an additional electric gimmick that kept the tank going even if all the house went kaput. Probably with batteries, that had to be replaced regularly. But, it was all such a joy, and we always noticed the goings on in that tank. Even Mayfly sat nearby and stared in, but never dared to put a paw inside. There was probably a net covering which prevented this.

When our son later on moved to an apartment near his college, he again got himself a fish tank, maybe not so large. Did he transport some of the fish in water filled plastic bags to the new abode?

Often when we visit a doctor's office that keeps a fish tank to entertain the waiting patients, or go to an Italian restaurant that has a super big fish tank near the tables, we are reminded of the tank of fish that kept our home busy years ago. Still do not know the accurate names of some of them, but we do recognize the colors, sizes, styles of all of them.

Well, speaking of fish, it should be mentioned once more, in case the reader has been distracted by the interesting fish tank paragraphs, that actual outdoor fishing with rods and reels and strings and lures was the hobby for both father and oldest son. When father grew much older, some of the old-fashioned rods and reels that were stored uselessly in the garage, were happily handed over to the actively fishing young adult son. They all used to catch snappers in the nearby Sound and sometimes collect hermit crabs. But one day we had a phone call from our oldest son who had been fishing way, way out on the inlets of the Atlantic Ocean, out east from where we lived. Come meet me soon for lunch near to you, he said, and please bring along another big storage ice box. Okay, so we hastened and went to the nearby diner. There he had driven his car and was opening the trunk to show us many big fluke laying on ice. Take a few for your ice box he insisted. We all went in to have a quick lunch. Then he had to drive all the way home to New Jersey quickly, with the other big flukes covered with ice.

We heard later on that he and his wife had delicious baked, or barbecued fluke for a few days. We took ours home, father cleaned the fish, and we baked ours, not being barbecue fans any more. Many years ago we used to go camping near oceans, catch fish, make fires in the rocky outdoor fireplaces with old pieces of wood we collected along the beach, and then barbecue our supper. That was a real natural way to live.

So now the Goldfish and Kittens story is almost over. If any reader wants to add stories, or decorate these fumbling memories more colorfully, welcome.

This Goldfish and Kittens, you might recall, is a sequel to my former tale called Sparrows and Puppies. Ain't nature grand.

My Button Box is Full

Buttons and Buttons and Buttons Galore

Threads and Needles and Basting the Holes

Trying to Fit Buttons into their Buttonholes

Close up the Coat and Go Out in the Cold

Come in and Sit Down and Manage the Keys

Push the Right Buttons, Oh Darling, Please, Please

Pushing More Buttons

Again this is happening, and I am really so very glad that I am now living in the age of buttons and more and more buttons. No, you nice older ladies, unfortunately I am not referring to the many colored and many sized buttons that we used to enjoy sewing on to our blouses and coats and sweaters, in the days that we really did make our own clothing on our old Singer sewing machines, or maybe just by hand. We did have boxes filled with these buttons, so when one fell off of some clothing, we could delve into the button box and search for a matching substitute button, or at least a button that would harmonize well with the other buttons. I guess we were always trying to fit in. Yes, that is the philosophical conclusion of how we older ladies used to be.

That was a long time before the present age of buttons that distresses me no end. All the technicalities, of buttons to push, on our computers, on our iphones, on our routers, and we have to now find out what that word router means. We have to know all this button stuff because otherwise we become completely cut off from family and from news of the world, and even from use of our telephones, if we have any of those. This morning, as usual, after a hearty breakfast, I sat down on my padded chair next to my desk and my computer screen. I wanted to read what my family members and some of my good friends had communicated to me recently. No such thing could happen, and now, many hours later, no such thing is happening. I couldn't access e-mail nor could I access the Internet to find out which country was at war with which country since I had last been informed the day before. I could not find out which movie star divorced which other one, and which baseball team had won over which other baseball team. Most distressing to me, and I am being satirical in case you don't catch on, I could not find out what the President of the USA had said when he traveled to which state to raise money. I wanted to know. Yes, I was crying about all this stuff.

So, lo and behold, on my computer screen there appeared a message in bold print and colorful background that if I wanted to get this all fixed, I should press a certain button, which I did, and then more words about what possibly could be wrong, and then I had to press the word NEXT to go on with the sermon, which I did. Eventually the final page of this biblical invective appeared and there were checks, not money checks but just little grimacing checks, next to what the problem could be. So I pressed another NEXT and was told to pull out some plus from some device and then wait a minute and see if lights went out or lights went on, etcetera. This kind of electrical know how was completely beyond me. So I called in my husband, a retired Physics and Computer Professor. He had to then go through all those page by page messages on the screen, and then he decided to pull a certain plug. Nothing happened, except that when we picked up the telephone receivers on all three of our telephones, they were all also dead.

Gratefully I have discovered, half a day later, when no E-mail works and no Internet works, and no telephone works, that my Open Office Writer does work. Guess this is because the Writer needs no complicated bunch of buttons to let me sit down and express my frustrations, which are infinite by now. Why even bother with a Word or a Writer on any structure such as a computer, anyhow. All I needed, to accomplish the same thing, was to pull out a pen and one of my numerous pads, and then write and write and write. I am old enough to know how to write in script, which was taught me as a child, when this excellent discipline involved push pulls and ovals which if not perfectly slanted, had to be repeated again. I am told that nowadays script is not taught in elementary schools, just printing, and so when I send a letter to a grandchild I must now only print the words. This, for me, is agonizingly time consuming. I often cannot decide whether to print or sign in script, the closing words of: love, from Grandma Mitzi

However one lets the words get out onto some surface or other, a computer screen or a paper pad, at least it does let off some of the steam of frustration. I still have no e-mail. I still have no World Wide Web of information. I still have no telephone. Half a day has gone by since this button problem of mine occurred. Incidentally, my HP printer is also defunct, so I am unable to print all these words onto a real piece of paper, so I could perhaps send them on to the higher ups in the bureaucracy that controls my life. So, turns out that I again made a rotten choice. I should have taken out my pen and paper pad and written all these steamy words in script.

Buttons Confuse Me

Not the first time my desperation in trying to use all those computer buttons had led me to express myself in words to my selfless, anonymous computer. I at least did have that secure feeling that I could talk to friends or others via my Email. This had worked for many years, and by just clicking twice on my Email button the messages in the Inbox were available, and also a Compose button enabled me to write new messages to whoever I wanted to, who also had a functional Email. I could Reply or forward the Emails that I clicked to appear on my screen. Well, today my life has changed, and an insurmountable snag keeps occurring everytime I want to merely click twice on my Email button. Mr. or Mrs. Google now puts up a big screen question, with photo of a messaging device, and just asks me to enter my: Name and then my Password. So I did it once, and in tiny red letters underneath it tells me that the name or password are not correct. What do you mean not correct? I have been using the same for several years. I surmise that Mr. or Mrs. Google is trying to intimidate me to buy some of their new-fangled apps., or visits, or whatever. Which they know I will never do. They know because they are constantly spying on all my Email messages and through magnificently complex software, they have put together more knowledge of my identity, preferences, dislikes, moods, tendencies, spelling errors, word fluency, etcetera, etcetera, than I myself will ever understand about myself. They will not let me use my Email anymore, and they know that now all my friends and family will try to send me Emails and will never know what happened when I do not respond.

I tried different passwords, none worked, and I shut down the computer for a few hours and tried again. Same stuff happened. I am admittedly very miserable about all of this. It is unfair, and especially since I am of the female gender, and more especially since I am an elderly woman, almost 85 years old. I will not succumb and will soon report the problem to someone, but to whom? Talking about all this helps me let off stressful steam, but does not solve anything else.

Now I will see if I can print this out. Probably my Printer has also been destroyed. We shall see. I keep my rambling down to only one page, however everyone knows that I write so profusely that usually there are three or more pages to get printed. We shall see.

Buttons Finally Explained

Perplexed and annoyed all day, because whatever buttons I pushed, in whatever order pushed, nothing worked. My telephone was dead, my computer only repeated the same instructions over and over, to push this button, then that button, then go on to NEXT and then find what wire to unplug, and then, only silence and non functioning followed. I could not find out anything from the Internet, and worse of all, could not communicate with family or friends. I could merely talk and talk to myself about how frustrating this was.

We were feeling triumphant that when we entered our car and then turned the key into the on button and then put feet onto the chug a chug or whoa just stop fast buttons, these all did work well as usual. So we could escape the non functioning devices in our house and drive elsewhere. Drive to a store that could give us milk, cheerios, a place to have our camera buttons entered and shiny colorful prints extruded, a place where we could talk to people in real actual life. We had taken along our cell phone. A phone that could magically connect to family members if held tightly in the cells of our hand and then had, you guessed it, the proper buttons pushed, and in the proper order. We thought that if we tried to connect with unseen buttons far away, in another state of the union, perhaps we could rise above the button problems in our place. Luckily this did work out, so we could at least talk fast to a few family members and explain that we were really okay, and laugh to ourselves because we were far from okay, and that they just could never evermore communicate with us by telephone or computer message because those means were no defunct. We could not give any lengthy explanations but did send our love to all.

We drove back to our house, because we had to do so, because we had left our dog there, and also had left a few other items there, like our furniture, our refrigerator with food inside, our clothes closets, and a sweater that still had a few missing buttons on it and had to have matching buttons found from the box of assorted buttons so buttons could be sewn on with needle and thread before the weather got very chilly and the sweater would be needed. Luckily it was a very nice sunny day, because we were sure that the next problem would be loss of electricity, as had happened during some past stormy days.

However something dramatic did happen. When we turned a corner to enter the street adjacent to our house, there were two gigantic official looking trucks parked face to face. Stop I cried to my driver. Look, one is carrying a huge new telephone pole. The other has a gentleman driver still sitting high up in his driver seat, as if transfixed, silently. Look, look, it is a FIOS truck. See the printing on the side of the truck. Not in script, but easily understood. Get out of our tiny by comparison car please, and ask that silent truck driver what is going on.

He said that during the night some car had crashed into the pole on the local avenue and knocked over all the pole and all its connections to all the wires that carried all the zoom on and zoom off messages to all the houses that depended upon FIOS. We told him that we lived nearby and asked him if perhaps that explained our frustrating loss of workable buttons. He agreed. He also offered the statement that it would take a very long time to remove the broken pole and all the connections that controlled everybody buttons for us. Then it would take these two helpful trucks a long time to put up the shiny unsplintered new huge pole on the local street and replace the shattered one. Not all. Then other technical men must arrive and push myriad buttons of their own in order to properly connect all the wires to make them work as heretofore. We were pleased to have all this verifiable news at last. Now we had a very plausible explanation.

We did not know what had caused that awful crash of car into the large village poll or if there was an error on the part of the driver of that car. Was that car driven by a drunk driver or did a driver have to swerve to avoid another drunk driver or did the car of the driver suddenly malfunction and its buttons get pushed in the wrong order or just stop working or worked too quickly or parts of that car or parts of that driver of the car or parts of the passengers in that car malfunction. A deep gloom descended when we imagined the crash victims and their fate. We were puzzled but expected that the next day a local newspaper would describe what happened. At least it all gave a full day or two or three or ten days of necessary employment with heavy telephone polls and wires now to the FIOS truck drivers and the FIOS technicians. This surprise and true ending to our own button problems was a relief.

It has not solved our button problem on telephone or button problem on the computer as yet. It is past overnight. At least I can type away printed words that make me feel smart. At last we can understand the issue. We know what caused the frustrating button loss. We doubt that once lost anything can be easily found again. We will continue to look for all the dropped buttons once dawn breaks and it becomes another sunny day. Before the rains return. AMEN

Focus On The Image Not The Now

In our minds we always have images, memories, an ever-changing encyclopedia of past events, how people looked and talked, scenes which are constantly embellished as we sometimes unexpectedly have them pop up, while awake, certainly while half asleep or just awakening, and all these images are forever there. We do not seem to have any control of thumbing through these images, except that rationally we can expect them moreso in some situations. Distances have a lot to do with all this. If a person we knew was in our life many years ago only, the images become more and more influenced by our particular current situations. We tend to sort out the good from the bad. The various appearances of such images changes with our moods, our motivations, our other experiences from time to time.

If the person or scene is very recent however, and there is a very temporary departing and returning, then other factors come up. Like being allowed only 20 minutes to perform an allegro and another 20 minutes for the legato, and only 10 more minutes for the final chorale. There is a strong time pressure and images are forced upon us in rapid succession, like squeezing the mint flavored toothpaste out of the tube before breakfasting and boarding the train for work.

If your long time, elderly husband is leaving the home for just one week-end, then there is only a brief time that you are alone. The actual dependencies, annoyances, routines that you and your long-time husband are used to following daily, have only a few moments to disappear from your vision now. The medical appointments, the *hurried shopping for groceries, the wish for more silly conversation, the early morning look of shuffling slippers and a bathrobe for breakfast appearance, the slowness of putting on his shoes and the inevitable misunderstandings, along with the appreciated way of both filling in forgotten names and dates for each other's drifting away recollections, all the usual hours of current, now hourly views of each other when both retired elderlies live so close, all these items catalogued above, have to exit quickly from the current theatre as if a fire alarm mistakenly was sounded. The details of the now daily life rush away swiftly, pushing everyone and everything out of the way.*

At last the old never to be forgotten images pop up, magically. As one lies down the visions of the early years appears. A smiling and gracious and handsome well-dressed, yet in casual attire, man stands nearby. It is your long-time husband, when he walked swiftly towards you and asked you to dance with him. His slow and rhythmic waltz while gently holding your arm and his arm quietly pressed upon your back, guiding you about the room. The melodies return in your images and you find yourself swinging from side to side along with him.

While alone that week-end and standing in your kitchen to put together a small plate of salad for yourself, you find yourself stalling to cut up the greens, with knife suspended for a while, as your eyelids close for a moment and before you is the scene of when you two traveled together up to countrified places, and stopped at a campsite. You stared fixedly at the kitchen window in front of you and saw instead the campfire being built by him, he tall and bending and placing twigs and then branches and then big found logs in airy pyramids while you were bringing the food to the outdoor wooden table and could sense the campfire smoke starting to rise and whirl nearby. Then he sat near to you and we were talking and singing together and planning where we would drive the following free day. Your head bows down low now in the kitchen and you finish cutting up your meager salad greens and you pour out some hot coffee and sit down at your maple table. As you munch slowly, the huge strong image then blasts upon you. You and he were watching the campfire go down slowly and you and he went into your camping trailer. His shoes and all came off quickly and he offered to help you discard your camping clothes. Without words then and without words as you experience this image, your night went on in the darkness. In the now of your kitchen, your eyes opened once again, and you stumbling put your salad plate and half finished coffee cup into the sink.

Home alone towards evening you put on some music on the radio in the den, and being increasingly lonesome, you force yourself to get up from the couch and dance around to the rhythm of the show tunes being played. You needed to exercise and most of the usual work of cooking a big dinner, and washing up extra laundry, and clearing numerous platters of food, and clunking the dishes into the dishwasher, all these usual routine actions were eliminated. Now as if living alone. So you danced in the den, with your companion doggie there as usual, and tried to keep cheerful for a while. Then very early to bed, because your long-time hubby who liked to stay up later and with the light on start to read one of his books which tended to keep you there or if trying to go to bed earlier you are annoyed and grimly shaking your head because you still had to see that light on. And having to step towards him once more to remind him to take his evening pill and change to pajamas already. Now alone at home, you could respond to your own natural routine, unencumbered though lonesome, with only your companion doggie for company. As you prepared for bed, you talked at length to your dog, whose ears showed she was listening. You described the weather to her and asked if she liked to run in the snow tomorrow. Her fluffy tail would wag showing her understanding and happiness. She was always the person in the house who did understand and respond to your talk and moods. But she did sniff around the other rooms in the house more than usual, realizing that he was not there tonight.

Your images of decades of earlier years floated next to you as you gradually fell asleep. The night's closeness, the grasping of a warm body, the rising exhilarating sensations and emotions, all returned as if still real in your isolated but imagined images now. The enjoyment of those years together when after raising their children well to their own adulthood, you two could return to the early days alone together, deciding where to go, what to do, how to make your own scenery as you wished. In the middle of the night alone, often wake up and be smiling softly to herself, probably because of the intensity and freshness of the images that were encased in her dreams. In early morning she jumped out of bed as usual, washing up and getting ready to make a hot breakfast for two.

Then reality set in, and she could hesitate and think of her personal ideas for spending this last day alone, of what she really wanted to do and had neglected to do for too long. She could easily concentrate on details without the burden of everyday chores, of who amongst her friends now and her friends long passed away she wanted to talk to, to inquire of, to portray older years for. Then she slowly went to make her breakfast and feed her doggie in the kitchen. She missed that she herself had to find the kibbles and biscuits which were usually there already, placed by her hubby, who had usually then gone back to sleep some more. She did all this and actually felt proud that she had managed the other day by herself so well. She was very cheerful as she felt she was returned to the independent self she had been when single many years ago and she found old thoughts and interests that had been buried in the long time overlay of married life.

She realized that many other people her age were now always in such situations, living alone after decades of shared days. So she thought more sympathetically about how some of her friends endured and yet created active lives, this ability to cope was a part of life. She could be strong and courageous and inventive as these images showed.

She had phone calls from him while he was away and from family he was visiting with, and his voice now was like her image of the younger years. He stood before her tall and laughing and never bent, slow or grumpy. After the calls she went to see herself in the mirror above her dresser. She smiled and combed her hair again and she did not see any facial wrinkles or frowns. She flexed her shoulders and tossed her head from side to side and then giggled to herself. It was quite wonderful, and the images of yore lightened up her look now.

By the last day he was away all changed for her. Anxiety of a sort grew within her as she went about preparing for his return. She was busy cleaning things, every piece of laundry washed, and she made three loaves of her home-made breads which she enjoyed concocting original recipes for. In other words, the past images were flushed away by the realistic and welcomed need to get ready for the actual return of her usual current life. When he did return safely, she was relieved and their doggie ran around wagging her fluffy tail and sniffing to find out where he had been all those days. I did know, but doggie certainly had more intimate sensations of the weather, the food, the other people, the scenes of where he had been. He also was immediately happy to pat his doggie and talk a big hello to her. He also said how are you to me. And so that is where my story ends. If the now becomes more irritating and disturbing as would inevitably occur again from time to time, I told myself to just focus on the images, not the now. Yes, focus on the images and not the now.

I could appreciate more than ever before all the good things he does and having a real person to talk to, to complain to, even to slowly dance with again. I had taught myself a way of focusing on the images, not the now. It was useful, because in a short while annoying incidents occurred again. I wanted to hear lengthy descriptions of what the family had been talking about, what the table settings were, how the food tasted, what happened in the airports. The experiences of traveling away for that week-end. But the usual silence or hand waving to substitute for lengthy paragraphs followed. I wanted to hear loads of praise for my home-baked breads, not just a succinct comment that the slice was good. As frowns solidified on my brow I told myself once again to just focus on the image, not the now. It more or less worked. In a few more hours he did do the very welcomed things, like pick up the mail in the village post office, and though just home from travels, be willing to drive me to the grocery store for more new food and items to refill our pantry, while he had to linger in his car, reading a magazine. I focused on the good. As did my doggie always.

MGT

Multi-Tasking Guy

Once a multi-tasking guy said: "Rest longer in bed, dearest, I will prepare breakfast for us." My oh my. So he blithely went into their kitchen, humming to himself as he stared at the cabinets. Then he put the oatmeal into the electric percolator, got a white towel which he moistened in the sink, and bent over to wipe up the spilled coffee grounds from all over the floor. He stared for a moment at the white towel, wondering that it suddenly had dark clouds all over it. Tossed this in the kitchen sink. Then he hurriedly ran down to the garage because he heard a loud gurgling sound, and turned off the dashboard key and the start button which he forgot that he had left on so he would be able to quickly drive over to the shopping center to buy some lo fat milk which his wife preferred, clambered up the stairs and then found the bowls and cups used only for special company and in some crowded drawer with deft and swift fingers located plastic spoons, knives and forks which he quickly threw onto the blue checked special table cloth next to the porcelain bowls and cups and using orange paper napkins which said Happy Thanksgiving, he hastily opened the back door, but having forgotten the key or to leave the latch open, he scurried around the yard to the front door, and rang and rang that front door bell.

Not sure if the bell worked, since he rarely used it, he persisted in ringing and ringing.

Having heard this continual ringing, his dear wife then got up from resting in bed, and smiling approached that sound. With an inquisitive look on her well rested face she opened the front door, and was surprised to there find her hubby who boldly announced,

"Breakfast for two is ready, my dear."

Guess what happened next, or make up some cheerful ending that is not overly horrific.

MGT

Two Grey Doves

Today is the first really warm day, up to 50 degrees already. Such wonders outside today. I looked out the window at our little wooden box bird feeder that always sits on the deck outside. Usually just a sparrow, couple cardinals, some blue jays all winter. This morning first lands the aggressive but colorful blue-jay to gobble up lots of the seeds. The sparrow returns and sat for a long time nibbling seeds in the box. We were just finishing the first cup of morning coffee. There, in the wooden box, sit two grey doves. Large ones, and accommodating to each other. They enjoy all the seeds and grains and stay together munching away. They look almost identical, grey, but the little black dots on one of them seem more pronounced than on the other one.

Had enough finally and both flew across the yard to the big evergreen tree, flashing white from the undersides of their wings. So we had to look them up in our Bird Book. Sure enough, the Bird Book explained that the grey dove man and lady look almost identical, with only the guy having somewhat darker spots. So it was a happy couple and new to our bird feeder. With cardinals and other birds, there are distinct differences between the genders, and we could tell easily if it was the bright red male cardinal with big head gear, the lighter red with only small head gear, the female. Although sometimes they seemed to give each other a seed to eat, as if kissing.

We drove along the road later on to our destination, along Mill Pond Rd., past the art museum, towards where we cross the railroad tracks of the LIRR. Have to watch out for the red and white gate going down when a train crosses there. Nearby there is a large horse farm and I always watch for the two brown and white horses that are nibbling away on the snow covered grass together. Surprise again. This time when I gazed at the horse farm there were four horses that came swiftly galloping out of the stable along the grassy hill. They were all dark colored, almost black, and one had a light blue blanket over the back. Had never seen these four before.

But where were my usual two brown and white horses that stayed near to each other all winter long, I called them the duo horses. Slowly one of the brown and white horses came out but not the other. The one did not join that new group of dark horses. Just stood looking soulful, all by itself. What happened to the other brown and white friend that was there all winter long? A sigh.

Then on to our destination, a Staples store where I had to have a bunch of papers bound together into a book with spiral edging.

While I waited there, a tall man comes to the desk with a very young kid, a little boy about two years old at most. The kid is holding a cookie in one hand and sucking on it from time to time. The man places the kid nearby in a chair in front of a computer desk. Then the man is getting his order taken care of and I watch that little kid. Kid is holding the 'mouse' with his free hand and pressing lots of keys, pushing the 'mouse' around, and then again tapping to see all the changing images. Well, I thought to myself that kid will soon be able to teach his tall dad how to use complicated software programs.

So this warmer weather gave me two grey doves, four dark horses, and one Kid. Alas, minus one brown and white horse.

What surprises will await once temperature hits 70, then 80, then 90 this summer? I will no doubt just be staying indoors where my room is air-conditioned. The birds and the horses and the Kids will be on their own.

The Living Bird

I miss the lost art of lonely bird-watching
Replaced as it is now
By all those groups of well
Organized folk equipped with
Latest models of neat hanging binoculars
Assorted books to guide their eyes
And tape recorded bird songs done
For them by experts to conduct
The sounds they should perceive
I suffer greatly from the
Loss of solitude and from the
Loss of chance to fumble in
My way, to wander into woods
And hear a rustling and then
Feel my hopes arise as to the
Creature that might nest
There unaware and then to
Miss him catching only distant
Whirrs from corners of my eyes
While inward vision smiles
To form the spectacle within
Imagination sweet, a gorgeous yellow
Graceful bird less wide than long
From head to toe and sporting hats
Of pea green feathers mixed with
Purple threads and down his sides

A keen black stripe so clean it
Nearly cuts away the dazzling tail
Of orange specked with white
A most delightful bird
That undulates in flight
And hums Aida all day long
Until he tires of themes
To seek his slumber in some bush
I suffer greatly from the lost art of
Waiting for my bird in chill and dark
With no instrument to comfort me
Seeking to forestall the chance
Of missing him full view, my bird
Whose repertoire defies all
Nomenclature, yes whose whimsical
Adroitness might at any moment
Lead him once again to fly
In parabolic trance while
Whirling fast from side to side
If only to enhance his full
And happy feeling as he
Can't resist the soaring up
Of new tunes now
Of Turandot and later on
Some Wayfarer songs with disregard
For all the programmed bird tapes
A wicked warbler tricky and
Delightfully aloof, for even I
Who love this gleaming bird
And wait alone in woods
Of frequent damp with guideless eyes
Must once again create his image
If I hope to spot and watch
His brilliant yellow soars
In airy regions inhospitable to
Ornithology

Milicent G. Tycko

I suffer greatly from the
Lost art of lonely bird-watching
Wishing I could shake the
Premonitions numbing me of
Vigil stands in stillness thick
While vast winds slowly glide by
Containing eons of spent dust
Of old mosquito wings suspended in
Salt spray mixed with particles of
Ancient Egyptian clay
I wait alone as if
Realizing that groups of those
Who watched bearing well equipped knapsacks
Of compasses and glass and maps
Are gone long since, their lists of birds
With greenish films of mold
Are strewn on forest floors
Those lists so old and accurate
I wait with imbecilic stare
For my bird to gleam and sing
In irresistible delight.

M. Tycko

Water Play

This is best performed within the reader's imagination. A play to read. The setting is a dining-room with wan light streaming through the window. Simply furnished. A table. Two chairs. Wallpaper as in a Vuillard painting. A man sits reading a newspaper in one chair. Across from him sits a woman. She jumps up from her chair.

Woman speaking: Within the heart of thick cold waves dwell whitened fish and other pulsing life albinoed by the lightless prison in which they passively float. The ponderous waters bent by moon and earth contain these intact delicate creatures which anonymously cling to life much as fruitless hope flourishes midst doomed despair. The slamming tonnage of furious ocean in stormy mood, while railing sternly to disassemble sturdy ships, suffices not to crush this tiny life that easily would fill a hand with thousands were it scooped up from the deep. Nutrient microcosm in foamy folds of sea.

She remains standing quietly as man reads newspaper without looking up.

Woman speaking more softly: Fastidious creatures persist in their evolutionary dances within the surging sea, wearing colorless delicacy modestly. They cannot care if they are seen, and can not complain if occasion traps them in a trailing net's coarse fibers, or if a deep sea diver's bubble glass peers down their cartilaginous spines. (Crescendo) Numerically they win and man's intelligence in mighty brain struggles to manipulate centuries old accoutrements of verbal symbols merely to register and accentuate the wave's hidden life. In despair the outnumbered human mind can lick its wounds by contemplating all the variegated filmy protoplasm that fills the former habitat of man. The mind grasps solace a singularly human mood also in the creatures of the sky and earth that

73

compensate for gloom: our dusky moths and patterned butterflies and all the tiger-lilies of the fields and our humid canopies of green. We hold the figurative cool fishes in our hand with carelessness while listening intently for our birds.

She glances disinterestedly at man who turns the page of newspaper.

Woman speaking evenly: We recognize these songs as we can sing. Each of our dawns we wake to sympathize with feathered chatter, for we know they cannot stop, much as we must speak in endless circles with incessant murmurs, whether loudly to each other as on stage, or mumbling in poetic pathos quiet within ourselves. We churn and surge within as does the ocean, for the sybellant sea has left a few eyedroppers full of salty fluid remembrances in interstices locked inside our greying brains. Pain it is to feel and it is pain to recollect and we are very well imprisoned in this swollen sea-gorged rhythm, just as the whitened organisms dwelling colorless in waves.

She sits down again.

Woman speaking in tidal beat: My father called me darling as he bore his aging cage of bones encasing cancerous glands. Others heard their mothers lisp upon them tenderly with lips that rounded out in screams of pain or froze in hopeless grimaces behind the screen. So my brain now reels in gloom when forced to recollect love's losses and urged to penetrate the hypothetical sphere defined by future loss and pain. The rip-tide twirls and churns the rocks at beaches' edge, even as it does my thoughts, and makes of all soft strands of sand.

The man then looks up from his newspaper.

Man speaking nervously: Albeit magically the water remains hot within my cup, devoid of fish-like thoughts and momentarily craving only ground-up beans of humid green-canopied climes.

Woman speaking listlessly: Here's the instant coffee.

She is listening oft for birds.

End

MGT

As I saw them carry a box from some cars
Towards the fresh opened earth in front of me
I realized it really was

My father

And then a giant heavy log
Smote me painfully
Across my face.

immediately; appointments to keep, shopping to do, phone calls to make. His calm statement served to put it all in perspective, but it did annoy others who felt he was making fun of their compulsiveness...which he was doing.

His own real life, growing up as a child in a Russian shtetl, being brought to America as a ten year old by his widowed mother, along with his siblings, his having to immediately work at tough jobs to help pay for the needs of the family, child labor, his ability to laugh when he was forced to stand in a big vat of chocolate syrup and stir it to make a few bucks, or forced to carry heavy cans of paint and ladders to help his "goyish boss", some other "ganuf" who got well paid for the paint job, and his cradling of his main love of music and singing. As a young child, his talent and voice had made him part of an orthodox Jewish boys choir, traveling in and around Odessa, the black sea area in Russia. His talent triumphed when he grew up in this country, when he became the admired leader of a boy's choir in the well-known Orthodox shul in the big city in America. Everyone in that community of recent Jewish immigrants knew him with respect. They all studied to become American citizens as soon as they could. They all wanted their children to excel in school, which did happen. They all respected the teachers and were gleeful about their new home. They all had fear in the late 1930s, when the dark shades had to be put over the windows at night, so they would not be bombed, as their brothers were in Europe. It was a frightening premonition of World War 2.

So it was not the remark of a simpleton, when father said, "the only thing you HAVE to do, is die". He tried to fold his arms over everyone, and he knew who was who. He made mocking noises when people tried to gain sympathy over some minor disabilities. He laughed at the other senior citizens who constantly complained of all their aches and pains as they were taken by bus to the senior center and were fed and entertained and interacted there. He was satirical about all those 'poor little babies'. Compared to his nine decades, it had to be a joke. Yet they all did try to be his friend and looked up to him. His sense of humor twinkled and he had many Yiddish phrases to prove it. He was missed if he did not join their group. So Maureen had a background which made her feel confident. She could often say "I" when she described her wonderful attributes. She knew she did not come out of thin air. Historical eras and personal ones did mold her, though she preferred to feel independent of all this; she knew it would be a bright, sunny day tomorrow. So she could recall how she felt about death while taking comfort in this image of her strong father.

Milicent Germansky Tycko

Squiggles Later On

The weather was getting chilly and some acorns were falling from the oak trees. One dark night we heard strange shuffling and running sounds coming from the attic. This continued for a few days until we wondered what was up there disturbing the normal-quiet atmosphere up there. So we called up a man who does carpentry and painting for us, and he showed up with his helper one day. He opened up the outside wood of an entrance to the attic while his helper went up into the attic from indoors.

Guess what? When the helper held a long broom-stick into the attic, a very cute and energetic squirrel ran right along the stick. Then the man who opened up the outside wood also swept out some leaves and twigs that were matted together to make a nest.

The workers hid in the bushes and think they saw some squirrels run out of the outside opening. But maybe it was just birds flying out of a nest in the eaves. Anyhow....something did happen, we know, because from then on we never heard anymore of the shuffling and running sounds from the upstairs attic.

Someone who knows all about squirrels in attics told us that they like to nibble and bite the electric wires up there, to keep their pretty teeth nice and short. So then we called up the electrician men to check our attic wires. Sure enough there was a lot of damage to the soft coverings of many wires, so the electrician men had a big job up there to take out the bad parts and put in new good electric wires. We did not want to have any fires from old damaged wires. Can you blame us for that? We still have a sample of a well-nibbled wire to show curious children. Also, the electrician men found a few acorns up there. That made us think that there really were squirrels hoarding food for their warm winter nest in our attic.

Well we did miss the squirrel family. But not for long. One day we saw Mamma Squiggles perched on top of our roof and signaling with her tiny paws to the squirrel children, Bing, Bong, and Baby Doll. To tell them which trees to scurry up on and where they could store more acorns for Winter. One day I looked out my window and saw Squiggles scurrying up the big pine tree, looking very well fed and happy. When I go to the window and open the curtains, if she happens to be in the area, she promptly scurries up the nearest tree to say hello.

I have learned a few things. It is really not good to feed peanuts to squirrels right on your own porch. Then they decide to come into your attic. It is better to say hello to them when they live in the wild, on the lawn, on the trees, running across your driveway.

I have to go now, because I think I will look out the window and wait to see Squiggles again.

End of Story

MGT

Printed in the United States
By Bookmasters